F[illegible]

AND FRENCH

Pam Bourgeois

KOLIBRI LANGUAGES

TABLE OF CONTENTS

COOKING TALES

La Tarte Tatin

Two sisters have the central role in this tale of the accidental discovery of a dessert that became a French classic.

In the late 19th century, the hotel opposite the station at Lamotte-Beuvron in Sologne was run by Stéphanie and Caroline Tatin, known locally as *les demoiselles Tatin*. It was a hotel that was popular with hunters who appreciated the quality of the food.

One day during a very busy period, one of the sisters (legend has it that it was Stéphanie) returned to the kitchen and was surprised to see that the dessert hadn't been made. She apparently saw a few peeled apples and quickly buttered a deep-sided pie dish, added sugar, cut the apples into chunks, placed them in the dish and put the dish in the oven.

She realised her mistake a few minutes later. She hadn't lined the dish first with pastry. It was neither a pie nor baked apples. It was too late to do much, so she quickly added a thinly rolled layer of pastry over the top of the apples and popped the dish back in the oven.

COOK'S TIP

Une Tarte Tatin is a great way to use up late apples. The juice of these apples can be rather tart and would sink into the pastry of a traditional pie. In a *Tarte Tatin*, the juice blends with the butter and sugar, making a delicious caramel.

The problem was how to serve it. Ever creative, the sisters placed a plate over the pie dish and turned the whole thing upside down. The apples, sitting in their caramel sauce, could now be seen. The dessert was immediately popular and the sisters made it time and again.

It is said that the fame of the dessert increased after the owner of the famous Parisian restaurant Maxim's tasted it

▸ JE VAIS PRENDRE LA TARTE TATIN, S'IL VOUS PLAÎT.

when dining at the Hôtel Tatin. Immediately impressed, he added the dish to his restaurant's menu. In 1926, Curnonsky, the famous French epicure, also introduced the dish to Paris and called it, in honour of its creators, *la Tarte des demoiselles Tatin*.

≡ It's not really clear how much of the origins and early fame of this dessert have been romanticized, but the Hôtel Tatin still exists, and in mid-September every year *la Tarte Tatin* is celebrated in Lamotte-Beuvron.

≡ Unlike most French desserts, *la Tarte Tatin* is served hot or at least very warm. Purists serve it without cream, ice-cream or any other trimmings.

La crème Chantilly

≡ *La crème Chantilly* became famous in the 18th century. It was prepared in the sumptuous dairy of le prince de Condé, owner of the château de Chantilly. The cream was served as an accompaniment to ice-creams and fruit for the many nobles who were guests at the château during open-air *fêtes*.

≡ Vatel, legendary pastry cook and caterer and *le maître d'hôtel* of le prince de Condé, is often credited with creating this sugared, whipped cream and bringing it to everyone's attention by serving it at a banquet given for Louis XIV at the château de Chantilly in 1671.

≡ The sumptuous feasts, hunting and entertainment prepared for the king and the court were spread over three days. The occasion was, however, blighted by the death of Vatel, who, having run short of meat one day and not receiving a delivery of fish in time the following day, considered himself discredited and committed suicide.

▸ LE CHÂTEAU DE CHANTILLY

≡ Some say that even the famous whipped cream was improvised when Vatel, running short also of cream, whipped the cream he had to give it more volume. This was certainly just part of the legend, as contemporary detailed records of the feasts do not mention whipped cream at all.

≡ Although Vatel is remembered as the creator of the famous Chantilly, it is probable that whipped cream existed already in Italy and was introduced in France by Catherine de Médicis following her marriage to Henri II. Who decided to add sugar to whipped cream remains a mystery.

≡ That the cream made at le prince de Condé's dairy became increasingly famous and was much appreciated is undeniable however. When served at Chantilly, long after Vatel's death, it elicited praise from nobles, such as la baronne d'Oberkirchin. In the middle of the 19th century, recipe books linked the cream, Vatel and the château. The cream had become forever associated with Chantilly.

≡ *La crème Chantilly* is made by whisking chilled liquid cream, *la crème liquide*, with vanilla, *la vanille*, and icing sugar, *le sucre glace*, until the cream thickens. It is ready as soon as the cream retains its wave shape when the whisk is removed. French chefs call this technique *monter en Chantilly*.

COOK'S TIP

It is preferable to use chilled cream and a cold bowl and whisk when whipping up a *crème Chantilly* to ensure that the cream doesn't simply become butter!

LA QUICHE LORRAINE

≡ *La quiche lorraine* originated in the department of Lorraine, in the east of France. At the time, the region was part of Germany, and the word *quiche* comes from the German 'kuchen', meaning cake.

≡ Recipes for making *la quiche lorraine* have existed for a long time. The dish was already popular in 1550, when it was frequently served at the court in Nancy, the capital of Lorraine, where it was much appreciated by le duc de Lorraine, Charles III.

≡ At this time, *la quiche lorraine* was made from bread dough, *la pâte à pain*, which was covered by a mixture of eggs, *les œufs*, cream, *la crème*, small pieces of salted butter, *du beurre salé*, and chives, *la ciboulette*. The mixture was called *la migaine* locally.

≡ Made of simple ingredients, which rural peasants would have or could procure easily, *les quiches* were often baked in the village oven. These ovens were kept alight, to economise wood, while the different families in the village cooked their bread in turn. While the oven was lit it was possible to also cook a *quiche*.

≡ In the 18th century, Vincent de la Chapelle, chef to Stanislas, the King of Poland and Duke of Lorraine, changed the recipe by substituting short crust pastry, *la pâte brisée*, for the bread dough. Since then, this has been the preferred pastry for the dish, although some cooks use flaky pastry.

▸ VERSATILE AND POPULAR, *LA QUICHE LORRAINE* HAS A LONG HISTORY.

In the late 18th century, following the death of Stanislas, Lorraine was attached to France and *la quiche lorraine* quickly became popular in French households.

Some maintain that bacon, *le lard*, was only added as an ingredient in the 19th century. Others consider that bacon was used ealier, maybe even in the original recipe. Possibly the recipe varied from village to village.

COOK'S TIP

La quiche lorraine should be served warm or hot. It can be served as a starter, or for a buffet or light lunch. Mini *quiches* are often served with an *apéritif*. Cheese is not an ingredient in the traditional *quiche lorraine*.

Since the 19th century, the recipe has not really changed, although a huge selection of savoury tarts with varied ingredients are now available in bakeries everywhere. *La quiche lorraine* remains, however, a great favourite and a benchmark for all other quiches. It is even referred to by its French name in other countries. That's surely the sign of a dish that, while remaining a French classic, has become truly international.

LE CAMEMBERT

Le camembert is a well-known cheese, possibly the best-known cheese in the world. It comes from Normandy and is made from the milk of Normandy cows. There is even a village in Normandy called Camembert.

The origins of the cheese are more uncertain. Some say that Marie Harel, a farmer in Normandy, created the cheese in 1791, at the height of the Reign of Terror that followed the French Revolution. She then named the cheese after the village where she was born.

Others say *le camembert* existed already. There are references, in 1680, to certain fine cheeses made in the village of Camembert that could be purchased at the nearby market at Vimoutiers. In this version, Marie Harel merely improved an existing cheese.

Napoleon III also figures in the story. In 1863, while travelling near Camembert, he was allegedly given *un camembert* and was so delighted with it that he requested that the cheese be delivered regularly to Paris.

JUST SO!

When French people buy *un camembert*, they usually open the box and press the centre of the wrapped cheese with their thumb. This is to test the ripeness so that they can choose one as runny or as firm as they want.

▸ JUST RIPE ENOUGH!

What is certain is that in the 19th century, the question of how to transport this increasingly popular cheese to other parts of France arose. The solution was found in 1890 when an engineer suggested a small circular box made of poplar wood. Light and practical, it solved the problem, and *le camembert* had its distinctive packaging which is still in use today.

The success that followed led to the creation of several cooperatives in the area around Camembert. These organised the collection of milk from local farms and transported it to large dairies. *Le camembert*, with its creamy centre and soft, white rind, was soon sent all over France and also exported.

In 1909, the producers, worried about the cheese being copied, defined the characteristics of *le camembert*, including the production technique, weight, diameter and, most importantly, that it be made from unpasteurised milk from cows of the Normandy race who graze outside for at least six months of the year.

During the First World War, *le camembert* gained further renown as it was included throughout the war in the rations of French soldiers.

In 1968, *le camembert de Normandie* was granted the distinctive *label rouge*, and in 1983 it obtained *une appellation contrôlée*, a label guaranteeing the origin. This ensured that only a cheese that was produced in Normandy, following certain established criteria, could be called *un camembert*.

La Bouillabaisse

≡ *Quand ça bouille, tu baisses.* 'When it boils, lower the heat.' This is a modern version of the Provençal words for 'to boil' and 'to lower', *boui-abaisso*, that form the name of Marseille's famous fish soup.

≡ The dish undoubtedly evolved from a fish stew eaten in ancient Greece and brought to Marseille by the Phoenicians who founded the city in 600 BC. Marseille is still referred to as *la ville phocéenne*.

▸ A NOT-TO-BE MISSED DISH WHEN VISITING MARSEILLE

≡ Local fishermen used to make the dish after their day's fishing in *les Calanques*, deep, narrow creeks near Marseille. They would first heat seawater in large cooking pots on the beach. When the water boiled, they threw in any fish they would not be able to sell. Once the fish was cooked, they poured the stock, *le bouillon*, over stale bread rubbed with garlic. Then they ate the fish, usually accompanied by *une rouille*, a spicy sauce made with red peppers and garlic.

≡ Over the years, this modest meal for poor people was adopted and modified by the middle classes. In the late 18th century, the seawater was replaced by a flavoursome fish broth, made from small fish from the deep water among the rocks. It included ingredients such as *le safran*, saffron, *le fenouil*, fennel, and *l'huile d'olive*, olive oil. Then, as in the traditional recipe, a variety of larger fish were cooked in the broth. The fish were very fresh and cooked just enough so they didn't disintegrate.

≡ *La bouillabaisse de Marseille* is made from at least four different kinds of fish, such as *la rascasse*, scorpion fish, *le rouget*, red mullet, *le saint-pierre*, John Dory, *la baudroie*, monkfish, or *le congre*, conger. Potatoes are also cooked with the fish.

COOK'S TIP

When serving *la bouillabaisse*, you can give guests a soup dish as well as the traditional two dishes of broth and fish. Guests can then, if they wish, eat the two together in the soup plate.

≡ *La charte de la bouillabaisse*, a charter created by French chefs in 1980, details the recipe and the way the dish is served, the broth put into one dish and the fish in a second. The fish are served whole and only cut into pieces in front of the diners. *La bouillabaisse* is accompanied by *une rouille* and croutons. *Les moules*, mussels, or other *crustacés*, shellfish, are not included in a traditional *bouillabaisse*.

≡ The dish is usually served with a dry white wine or a powerful rosé wine from the Marseille region.

Le Baba au Rhum

≡ Legend has it that this popular dessert was invented in the early 18th century. Stanislas, the King of Poland and Duke of Lorraine, who also played a role in the story of *la quiche lorraine*, was given a traditional *kouglof* cake that he found too dry. He asked for a liqueur, most sources cite a Malaga wine, to be poured over it.

≡ The result became known as *un baba*, probably because a similar dessert existed already in Stanislas's native Poland. There it was called a 'babka', meaning 'old woman' or 'grand-mother'. It was a yeast cake made from eggs, milk and butter, cylindrical in shape and tapering to a point. It was prepared for religious festivals, particularly Easter.

≡ The idea that somehow the name came about because Stanislas had been reading The Thousand And One Nights, *Les Mille Et Une Nuits*, in which one of the heroes is Ali Baba, is charming but unlikely!

≡ In 1725 Stanislas's daughter married Louis XV. Nicolas Stohrer, who had been Stanislas's pastry-cook, and possibly the person who added the liqueur, followed her to Versailles as her pastry-cook. He added a confectioner's custard, *une crème pâtissière*, to *le baba* as well as currants, *les raisins de Corinthe*, raisins, *les raisins secs*, and saffron, *le safran*.

In 1730 he founded the Pâtisserie Stohrer, a shop that still exists today at 51 rue Montorgueil in the 2nd *arrondissement* in Paris. It is the oldest *pâtisserie* in Paris.

In 1835, one of Stohrer's descendants substituted rum for the liqueur and made *le baba au rhum* one of his specialities. It later became circular in shape, having adopted the ring shape of the *savarin* cake created by the brothers Julien, who were also famous *pâtissiers* at that time. *La crème Chantilly* was introduced too instead of confectioner's custard.

COOK'S TIP

Leave *le baba* to dry out a little after removing it from the cake mould. It will then soak up the rum completely. *Le baba au rhum* is eaten chilled and can be served with a red fruit salad.

Nowadays, *le baba au rhum* is usually circular and is generally filled with *la crème Chantilly*, although it can still be found with *la crème pâtissière* also. It is nearly always served in individual portions.

Alain Ducasse, the Michelin-starred French chef, has made *le baba au rhum* one of his signature desserts in his restaurants.

LE CASSOULET

The origins of this speciality from the southwest of France are fiercely debated. Basically a bean stew, the beans may have been introduced from the New World. Others say that the Arabs had already brought the beans to France in the 12th century.

One legend says that the dish goes back to the Hundred Years War when, in the besieged town of Castelnaudary, a huge stew was made from all the remaining food in order to feed the soldiers. Thus fortified, the soldiers overcame the English and freed the town.

Whatever its origin, the dish was a poor man's dish made from leftovers and cooked in the hearth or in the baker's oven for a long time.

There are three famous *cassoulets*, those of Castelnaudary, Carcassonne and Toulouse, often referred to respectively as the Father, the Son and the Holy Ghost of *cassoulets*. The question as to which is the most authentic has long been a source of argument. Around 1900, the question was even debated in a Parisian newspaper. In fact there are many varieties, as each village prides itself on its recipe.

There is general agreement, though, on the proportions in a good *cassoulet*. The stew should be made with at least 30% of meat, usually goose, *l'oie*, or duck, *le canard*, and pork, *le porc*, or mutton, *le mouton*. The remaining 70% should be haricot beans,

▸ NOW WHICH VARIETY OF *CASSOULET* IS THIS?

les haricots blancs (although broad beans, *les fèves*, were used originally), pork rind, *la couenne*, meat juices, *le jus de viande*, and herbs, *les aromates*.

Le cassoulet is cooked in the oven for a long time until the beans become soft. Traditionally, the skin which forms must be broken seven times while the dish cooks, and the spoon should stand upright in the dish when it is ready.

The word *cassoulet* comes from an old Languedoc word for an earthenware dish, *cassolo*, which, by association, became used for a dish cooked in the oven. It also comes from a Provençal word, *cassa*, an ancestor of the modern French word for a saucepan, *une casserole*.

Le cassoulet is served in an earthenware dish with a flat base and sloping sides that has been made for hundreds of years by the potters of Issel near Castelnaudary.

COOK'S TIP

Le cassoulet should be served piping hot with a red wine from the region, such as a Minervois or a Corbières. Portions are large and the dish is certain to create a convivial atmosphere on the coldest winter evening.

▸ CAMBRAI, A TOWN WHERE *LES BÊTISES* ARE APPRECIATED.

Les Bêtises de Cambrai

Quelles bêtises as-tu faites ? 'What stupid thing have you done?' This was the reaction when an apprentice at the confectioner's Depinoy in Cambrai, in the north of France, made an error in the recipe when making candies. Rather than letting his production go to waste, the sweets were put on sale on the shelf reserved for broken sweets sold by weight.

To everyone's surprise, the sweets proved extremely popular with clients, who asked specifically for *les Bêtises*. Today la Maison Depinoy still makes these candies and claims to have created them.

They are not the only ones to make this claim. The confectioners Afchain maintain that it was the son of the owner, Emile Afchain, who made an error and was scolded by his mother for his '*bêtises*'. He added mint by mistake and, rather than admit it, kept turning the mixture until it became white. Again the candies were put on sale and became popular.

It is possible that neither story is completely true. The sweets are probably linked

INTERNATIONAL FAME

In 1992, *les Bêtises de Cambrai* were recognised as part of the culinary heritage of Nord Pas de Calais. Every year 400 tons of the sweets are made.

to the important market that was held on the 24th of each month in Cambrai. Having sold their livestock, the farmers stayed on to *commettre les bêtises*, to do silly things, in this case spend their money. They often bought boiled sugar candies made for passers-by and cut into pieces with scissors.

La Maison Afchain gradually modified these sweets, adding Mitcham mint, beating the sugar to incorporate more air and introducing a strip of caramelised sugar to give the rectangular-shaped candies a distinctive appearance and sweeten them. *Les Bêtises de Cambrai*, the famous mint humbugs, or hard mint candies, were created around 1850. It was only from 1947 that they were sold individually wrapped.

The two companies continued to dispute the paternity of *les Bêtises* until, following a lawsuit, it was decided that la Maison Depinoy was to be recognised as the creator, and la Maison Afchain as the inventor. It was a subtle difference.

Today the sweets, made from natural products only, can be found with flavours such as raspberry, *la framboise*, chocolate, *le chocolat*, or orange, *l'orange*, as well as the traditional mint, *la menthe*. You can see them being made on site at, of course, either la Maison Depinoy or la Maison Afchain.

QUIZ

1. Are the following statements true or false?

a. *La quiche lorraine* was originally made with bread dough.
b. Mussels are an important ingredient in *une bouillabaisse.*
c. In the First World War, *le camembert* was included in soldiers' rations.
d. *Une Tarte Tatin* is served hot.

2. Find the French words in the jumbled letters.

a. *linavel* _ _ _ _ _ _ _
b. *grueto* _ _ _ _ _ _
c. *ucqihe* _ _ _ _ _ _
d. *rtohcai* _ _ _ _ _ _ _

3. Match the English word with its French equivalent.

a. *la ciboulette*	1. monkfish
b. *le bouillon*	2. raspberry
c. *la baudroie*	3. chives
d. *la framboise*	4. stock

Solutions on page 96.

THE FRENCH WAY

10 French Housewife's Tips

≡ The French have lots of tips for coping with minor problems when preparing meals. For example, they don't panic when they find that the avocados, *les avocats*, for the next day's starter are not ripe. They'll simply wrap each avocado in newspaper overnight. The following day they will be just right.

≡ When there is no salad spinner, *une essoreuse*, available, grandmother's ways will be remembered. The lettuce will be placed in a clean tea towel, and with the four corners held securely together, it will be shaken vigorously up and down. Any excess water will be removed. This is best done outside, though, to avoid a wet kitchen floor!

≡ No electric parsley cutter, *un hachoir*? After the large stems are removed, the parsley leaves will be placed in a teacup. The parsley can then be chopped easily inside the cup with a pair of scissors.

≡ To peel tomatoes, a French cook will place them for a few seconds in boiling water. The skin can then be removed easily with a sharp knife.

≡ To prevent milk from boiling over when heated, the trick is to place a dessertspoon in the bottom of the saucepan. No more cleaning up after a second's inattention.

≡ A salad in a dressing will only be tossed at the table when the guests are ready to eat. This stops the salad from turning brown at the edges and keeps it nice and crisp, rather than tired looking, *fatiguée*.

LANGUAGE CHECKLIST: FOOD VERBS

essorer une salade to spin a salad
faire des tranches to cut into slices
hacher du persil to chop parsley
touiller la salade to toss a salad
ajouter du sel to add salt

▸ *RÂTER UNE MAYONNAISE* IS NOT NECESSARILY A DISASTER.

≡ To ensure perfect slices of *pâté* or *foie gras*, French cooks will dip the blade of the cutting knife in a bowl of hot water before cutting the slices. The same tip works when serving ice-cream with a scoop.

≡ If a mayonnaise has separated because the oil has been added too quickly, the French cook will simply start a new mayonnaise and then, very gradually, add the first mayonnaise to it. It will mix perfectly and thus avoid waste.

≡ Too much salt in a soup or a sauce? A peeled potato,

cut in half, will be added. As the dish cooks, the potato will absorb the excess salt.

≡ And to cool that bottle of French champagne, a handful of cooking salt, *le gros sel*, will be added to the ice in the champagne bucket. This will accelerate the cooling process.

Serving French food

≡ The way food is presented is important to French people. Often presentation can reflect the quality of the food. A fish served whole, rather than filleted, will include the head to show that the fish is fresh.

≡ An attractive-looking dish shows knowledge and respect for the food. French cooks always try to aim for a pleasing visual effect. Two or three colours are used, but no more. The colours are preferably either complementary, such as oranges and reds, or contrasting.

≡ In terms of texture, each dish should, ideally, combine elements that are crisp, *croustillant*, and soft, *moelleux*, or melting, *fondant*. If everything feels the same when placed in the mouth, it quickly becomes boring.

≡ The way food is placed on the plate is often echoed by the shape of the dish. A round plate will have the food set around it, in a circular fashion, or in the middle. On a longer, narrow plate, the food will be laid out in a linear fashion.

≡ Herbs, spices, slices of fruit or vegetables are used to add a final touch. *Une gousse de vanille*, a pod of vanilla, will frequently top a dessert; *une tomate cerise*, a cherry tomato, sliced in half, a plate of pasta; and flowers, or a slice of an exotic vegetable, a salad. The visual effect combines well with the promise of different flavours.

To make soup look more interesting, a French cook will often decorate the surface of the soup with a little single cream, *la crème liquide*, in a simple pattern. Similarly for a sauce or salad dressing, a small brush is used. Dipped in the sauce, it can delicately decorate the plate. This artistic touch adds elegance.

When seafood is presented in the shell, a plate of ice is a traditional method for ensuring that the precious juices of *les huîtres*, oysters, for example, don't escape. It also ensures that a decorative presentation remains in place.

« On ne peut pas faire de cuisine si l'on n'aime pas les gens. »

Joël Robuchon

The presentation of dishes may vary depending on the context. Usually, for a family meal or when inviting friends, the food is presented in serving dishes, placed in the middle of the table for each guest to help themselves. Only for a more formal dinner, or for certain starters or desserts, will the dishes be presented separately for each guest.

Food Dos and Don'ts

≡ When ordering a coffee after a meal, do specify if you want milk in it. The French consider coffee with milk indigestible after a meal, and your coffee will automatically be served black unless you request otherwise.

≡ In a café you will usually be asked how you want your tea. The choice is often between black or lemon tea, *un thé nature* or *un thé citron*. If you want milk with your tea, ask for cold milk, *un peu de lait froid*, otherwise you may be served hot milk.

≡ Don't order or serve white wine after red wine. The French have a saying about the dire results of doing this. *Blanc puis rouge, rien ne bouge. Rouge puis blanc, tout fout le camp.* Roughly translated this means that nothing moves when drinking red wine after white, whereas when drinking white after red, everything goes haywire.

≡ Cheese is served before the dessert in France. In a good restaurant, the cheese will be placed on your plate

WHAT'S IN A NAME?

A dish of various raw ingredients is called *une salade*. However, French people also talk about *une salade* rather than *une laitue* when referring to the lettuce they are preparing for a meal or that they have picked in their garden.

in the order you should eat it, going from milder to stronger tasting cheeses. Don't keep cheese in the fridge, just in a cool place. If that's not possible, remember to take it out of the fridge an hour or so before serving it.

- If you are served lettuce, you should not cut the leaves, but instead fold them onto your fork.

- Bread is generally broken with the fingers, although some families will use a knife. You should then break a small piece off to eat it rather than biting into the whole piece. If using a piece of bread to sop up sauce on your plate, spear it on your fork to do so rather than holding it with your fingers.

- When served *foie gras* and toasted bread, place a small piece of the *foie gras* on the bread to eat it. Don't try to spread it by crushing it with a knife.

- It is considered good manners in many families to eat fruit, such as peaches, with a knife and fork. It's a tricky exercise and needs some practice. However, the French don't crush peas on the back of a fork to eat them and will be mystified if they see you doing so.

▸ ENJOY CRUSTY FRENCH BREAD WITH YOUR MEALS.

▸ FRENCH CHEFS HIT A HEAD OF GARLIC WITH THE FIST TO BREAK IT INTO INDIVIDUAL CLOVES.

5 FAVOURITE INGREDIENTS

≡ Garlic, *l'ail*, is immediately evocative of French cooking. When preparing a roast or poultry for even the simplest meal at home, a small cut will be made in the meat with a sharp knife and part of a clove of garlic will be inserted. There are various kinds of garlic, including the highly prized *l'ail rose de Lautrec*. Garlic is also an important ingredient in many regional dishes such as *l'aïoli* of Provence and *le tourin*, a garlic soup favoured in Gascony.

≡ *Le piment d'Espelette* is grown in the Basque region in the southwest of France. It is a variety of chili pepper and has a distinctive flavour as it is dried for a long time in the sun. However, it is no stronger than ordinary black pepper and is used instead of pepper in many Basque dishes, the most famous of which is the traditional chicken dish, *le poulet basquaise*. Festoons of dried peppers decorate many French kitchens and shops, particularly in the southwest.

In 16th-century France, cinnamon, *la cannelle*, was used in over half the recipes of the period. It remains very popular with French cooks and is often associated with apples and chocolate. Today French housewives not only use it in baking but also sprinkle it over savoury dishes. It is frequently used in herbal teas, *les infusions*.

Orange-flower water, often referred to as *fleur d'oranger*, rather than the more correct *eau de fleur d'oranger*, is a favoured ingredient when baking. It is obtained by a distillation of the petals of the blossoms from the bitter orange tree. It is used to flavour *madeleines* and *brioches* particularly, but also chocolate mousse and baked custard pies, among other dishes. French grandmothers often add it, with a little sugar, to yoghurts for a children's teatime treat.

Truffles, *les truffes*, are a luxury in France, and not everyone can afford them. They will be used sparingly and stored in the fridge next to the eggs, allowing the latter to absorb their perfume so that the next omelette will be special. Even if a whole truffle is beyond the budget, housewives will use truffle oil or truffle vinegar to impart that distinctive flavour to salads.

FOOD FACTS

Le piment d'Espelette was used in the production of chocolate in 17th-century France.

Truffles are expensive and are often called black diamonds, *les diamants noirs*.

Unlike other types of garlic, *l'ail rose de Lautrec* is sold in bunches.

Superstitions about dining

≡ *Placer le pain à l'envers sur une table.* French people take care, when placing bread on the table, to ensure it is the right way up. Apparently, in the past, if a prison guard placed the bread upside down on the table, it was a way of informing that prisoner that he was to be guillotined, hence the unlucky association.

« La table est le seul endroit où l'on ne s'ennuie jamais pendant la première heure. »

Anthelme Brillat-Savarin

≡ *Treize invités autour de la table.* Traditionally, 13 is an unlucky number, with the exception of *vendredi treize*: when the 13th of the month falls on a Friday, it is considered a lucky day, especially when buying tickets for a lottery. Thirteen guests around a table is something to be avoided, however, and the hostess will often add a 14th plate, or ensure there are two tables, just so there is no bad luck.

▸ TCHIN-TCHIN !

≡ *Renverser du vin sur la table.* If a person spills some wine, they should dip their index finger in it and rub it across their forehead, as this brings good luck.

≡ *Passer le sel de main à main.* Superstitious French people never pass the salt from hand to hand. If a neighbour at table requests the salt, you should pick it up and place it on the table rather than putting it directly in your neighbour's hand. In the past, salt was very expensive and so spilling it was to be avoided and considered bad luck.

≡ *Tchin-tchin !* is what French people often say as they raise their wine glasses and clink glasses with

each other. Historically this gesture used to be carried out more forcefully so that the liquid from one glass would spill into another. It ensured that no one put poison in a glass as it could end up in other glasses also.

≡ *Casser du verre blanc.* Dropping and breaking a glass accidentally is a sign, in France, of good luck, possible a happy meeting or unexpected money. However, to break a mirror is the opposite and to be avoided.

≡ *Mettre du sucre à la place du sel serait l'arrivée d'une bonne nouvelle.* This traditional saying is likely to reassure any superstitious French person who mistakenly adds sugar to a dish instead of salt. The good news they will receive as a result may compensate for the taste of the dish being a little strange!

Celebration food

≡ *Les dragées*, blue or pink sugared almonds wrapped in tulle and tied with appropriately coloured ribbon, are distributed at children's baptisms. For first communions and weddings, the *dragées* are white. Traditionally, the bride and groom were showered with *dragées* as they came out of the church. Nowadays, the bridal couple usually give their guests a small container with five *dragées* representing health, long life, happiness, fertility and wealth.

Elle l'a retourné comme une crêpe means she quickly got him to change his mind.

≡ *La pièce montée* is the traditional French wedding cake. It is made of caramelised choux pastry balls filled with confectioner's cream and piled into a pyramid shape. The whole is held together with spun sugar or caramel. Traditionally, girls of a marriageable age take a piece in the hope of finding a husband. The bride is usually given the first piece to encourage fertility.

≡ *Les treize desserts*, representing Christ and his disciples, are served at the end of *le gros souper*, a traditional meal eaten

▸ BE CAREFUL WHEN YOU BITE INTO THIS PASTRY!

before or after Christmas Eve Mass in Provence. The dishes vary from family to family but include almonds, raisins, hazelnuts and figs, known as *les quatre mendiants*, the four mendicants. There are also marzipan sweets, fresh fruit, nougat and pastries, such as *la pompe à l'huile* made with olive oil. The guests must eat a little of each dessert, all of which are then left on the table for three days.

≡ *La galette des Rois* is a puff pastry dessert filled with frangipane. French bakeries fill their shelves with *galettes* destined to mark Twelfth Night. They are so popular that most families buy them more than once! It's a fun tradition to *tirer les rois*, that is, to share the *galette* in the hope of finding the charm hidden inside. The person who finds the porcelain charm, called *la fève*, as it was originally a bean, in their slice becomes the king and must wear the golden cardboard crown given with the pastry. To make the game fair, the youngest person hides under the table and decides who gets the next piece while someone else cuts the pastry.

≡ Forty days after Christmas, *la Chandeleur*, Candlemas, is the day for eating thin pancakes, *les crêpes*. The shape and colour of *crêpes* evoke the sun, a symbol of light like the candles traditionally associated with this festival. Popular fillings are jam, sugar, salted butter or lemon. Tossing and catching a *crêpe* in the pan while holding a coin in one hand brings future prosperity.

Classic French dishes

Certain dishes are an essential part of French culinary tradition and are prepared as they have been for generations. They also remain the basis for new variations. The French talk about a recipe being *revisité*, meaning that the presentation, ingredients or cooking method are reinterpreted to give the dish a modern feel.

▸ *LE COQ AU VIN* IS ONE OF THE MOST TRADITIONAL OF FRENCH DISHES.

In the 16th century, Henri IV is said to have promised that every labourer in his kingdom would be able to afford a hen in his cooking pot. Hence *la poule au pot*, a classic dish made from a hen stuffed with vegetables such as carrots, onions, leeks and turnips and simmered for several hours. It became a popular choice in rural France for Sunday lunch.

Le navarin d'agneau printanier, as the name suggests, is traditionally eaten in the spring and is often the dish chosen to celebrate Easter. It is based on a shoulder of lamb and spring vegetables. The name probably comes from a recipe concocted by a French chef following a great naval victory, in 1827, at Navarin in Greece. It may also be a pun on the French word navet, meaning turnip, one of the ingredients.

La blanquette de veau is a veal stew. *Blanquette* refers to the way it is cooked, that is, without first browning the butter and the veal. Its association with the word *blanc*, white, means that this white meat is traditionally served with white rice and without any vegetables, as that would add colour.

HERE TO STAY

In 2010, *le repas gastronomique des Français* was recognised by UNESCO as part of the world's intangible cultural heritage. It is described as 'a festive meal bringing people together for an occasion to enjoy the art of good eating and drinking'.

Le coq au vin is one of the most traditional of French dishes. Although *un coq* is a rooster and the long cooking time renders tougher meat tender, it is often made with chicken. The meat is usually marinated the previous day and then braised and cooked with mushrooms, diced bacon, carrots and onions in a Burgundy wine.

▸ *UN POT AU FEU* IS PERFECT IN THE WINTER.

Le pot au feu is said to be the essence of French family cuisine. Its name comes from the cooking pot that used to hang in the hearth and in which meat, usually beef, and vegetables were cooked. The dish also provided a soup and could be added to over a period of days as some of it was eaten. It was a perfect meal for cold winter nights.

Food trends

≡ French chefs prize inventiveness and creativity, but they are not averse to borrowing from other cultures. American cookies and brownies are now found in French bakeries, although when requested by shoppers, there is a distinctive French pronunciation. Cupcakes have also crossed the Atlantic, with some *pâtisseries* specialising in them.

≡ Other dishes have been completely adopted. Traditional British fruit crumbles have become a staple of dessert menus in French restaurants. This is particularly surprising in a country where hot desserts are not common. Cheesecakes are also now trendy, *tendance*, although many French diners are still not quite sure what to expect when they order one!

≡ *Cocktails dînatoires* or *buffets dînatoires* are very fashionable. On these occasions, the food is more substantial than for the traditional *apéritif*, with its nibbles and a drink, but they are not full sit-down meals. Hot and cold food is served, with the emphasis on *le finger food*, items that can be eaten while standing and chatting to business contacts or friends.

TIPS FOR DIPS

Dips are becoming popular in France, and traditional vegetables can add variety and originality. Black radishes, peeled so that there is a very fine black rim when cut in thin slices, are perfect for dipping.

▸ NOWADAYS, CRUMBLES ARE SO FRENCH!

Les verrines have become popular in recent years. These are small glasses in which little portions can be served and eaten with a spoon. Served in homes as starters and in restaurants as appetizers, they are particularly popular in *les buffets dînatoires* as they allow tasty and original creamed or pureed food to be eaten easily. They are also very decorative and colourful.

Les légumes anciens, traditional vegetables, many of which have not been included in dishes for generations, have made a big comeback. They are now sought out by French chefs and given prominence in their latest recipes. *Les panais*, parsnips, were unknown in French vegetable shops until recently. They can now be found easily, as can *les rutabagas*, swedes, *les topinambours*, Jerusalem artichokes, *les crosnes*, Chinese artichokes, and *les radis noirs*, black radishes.

Did you say hamburgers? Yes, the French have now invited hamburgers into their kitchens. Even some of the most famous chefs have devised gourmet hamburgers, adding some very French ingredients, such as fennel or blue cheese. Restaurants specialising in *les hamburgers gourmands* are very 'in', particularly in the chic areas of Paris. Now the French are even beginning to talk of *le street food* without disdain.

QUIZ

1. Match the first half of the name of the dish with its second half.

a. *Une poule*	**1.** *de veau*
b. *Une blanquette*	**2.** *au feu*
c. *Un pot*	**3.** *d'agneau*
d. *Un navarin*	**4.** *au pot*

2. Fill in the blanks using the verbs below.
éviter, inviter, renverser, casser, passer

a. *Il ne faut pas* __________ *le sel de main à main.*
b. __________ *du verre blanc porte chance.*
c. *Il faut* __________ *de placer le pain à l'envers.*
d. __________ *du vin sur la table porte malheur.*
e. *Il vaut mieux ne pas* __________ *treize personnes à diner.*

3. Fill in the missing letters to complete the words.

a. *une ess_ _ _ use*
b. *une _ _ _ ffe*
c. *une in_ _ _ ion*
d. *une _ _ _ ette*

Solutions on page 96.

TALKING ABOUT FOOD

Expressing food preferences

When invited by French friends or when eating in a French restaurant, you may need to state your preferences as far as food is concerned. Sometimes this will just be a simple question of which drink or food you would prefer. When answering, don't forget to add a polite *s'il vous plaît*.

Qu'est-ce que vous prenez ? Your host may ask this when serving *un apéritif*. You can reply simply by giving the name of the drink: *Un whisky, s'il vous plaît. Un pastis, s'il vous plaît. Un verre de vin blanc, s'il vous plaît.* A glass of white wine, please.

You can use the expression *je préfère* to say that you prefer a fish or a meat dish. *Je préfère le poisson. Je préfère le coq au vin.* If you're a vegetarian, you can say, *Je préfère un plat végétarien, s'il vous plaît.*

When you need to say the degree to which you want something cooked, you can use the same verb. You may be asked whether you want the meat rare, *saignante*, medium rare, *à point*, or well done, *bien cuite*. You can reply, *Je préfère bien cuite*.

LANGUAGE CHECKLIST: PREFERENCES

Je préfère...
I prefer...
Je préfère sans...
I prefer without...
Je voudrais...
I would like...
Je suis désolé...
I'm sorry...
Je ne mange pas...
I don't eat...
J'aime beaucoup...
I really like...

When you want to exclude a particular ingredient such as cream, sauce or cheese, you can continue to use *je préfère*. *Je préfère sans crème. Je préfère sans sauce. Je préfère sans fromage, s'il vous plaît.*

However, when you want to specify a preference when purchasing food, use *je voudrais*. *Je voudrais une baguette bien cuite.* I would like a baguette that is well baked. *Je voudrais un gâteau avec de la crème Chantilly, s'il vous plaît.*I would like a cake with whipped cream, please.

At times it can be important to be diplomatic and nuance what you say so that you don't sound rude. This is particularly true when you want to refuse something. You can start by apologising, *Je suis désolé*, and then add that you don't eat snails or frogs' legs. *Je ne mange pas les escargots. Je ne mange pas les cuisses de grenouilles.*

When you want to express a strong preference for something, you can use *j'aime beaucoup*. *J'aime beaucoup le cassoulet. J'aime beaucoup le poisson.* When you really like something, you can say, *J'adore le chocolat !*

▸ JE PRÉFÈRE LA VIANDE BIEN CUITE, S'IL VOUS PLAÎT.

French food courses

Les amuse-bouches, sometimes called familiarly les amuse-gueules, are small, dainty dishes served before the starters in some restaurants. Literally translated, this means something that keeps your mouth happy!

Starters are called *les entrées*. In the *à la carte* section of most menus, there is a choice of hot and cold dishes, *les entrées chaudes* and *les entrées froides*. French family meals used to be very long and elaborate with *une entrée froide* followed by *une entrée chaude*. Nowadays it is usually one or the other, except for big events or in expensive restaurants.

The main dish is called *le plat principal* or sometimes simply *le plat*. It will be a fish dish, *un plat de poisson*, or a meat dish, *un plat de viande*. It will usually be served with vegetables, *les légumes*, which are sometimes referred to as *la garniture* or *l'accompagnement*.

« Dans certains restaurants, on appelle "plat du jour" les restes de la veille qui ne peuvent pas attendre le lendemain. »

Philippe Bouvard

The cheese course follows the main dish and precedes the dessert. The choice is generally between the cheeseboard, *le plateau de fromages*, and *un fromage blanc*. The latter is a smooth mixture of drained milk curds, served with cream, to which you can add sugar. The waiter may simply ask, *Fromage sec ou fromage blanc ?*

- The dessert course comes next. The desserts may be presented on a dessert trolley, *le chariot de desserts*, or you may be asked to select one from the menu. The selection usually includes *les desserts glacés*, made with ice-cream or frozen cream, and traditional desserts, such as *une crème caramel* or *une mousse au chocolat*.

- *Les pâtisseries*, such as *un baba au rhum* or *une tarte aux fruits*, will also be a dessert choice.

- Sometimes desserts are called *les entremets*. *Les entremets* used to be dishes served between the main course and dessert, hence their name. Gradually these dishes became sweeter until they became just like desserts. Nowadays the word just means desserts but excludes *les pâtisseries*.

- Coffee is served after the dessert in France. It may be accompanied by a selection of *petits fours* or other treats. These will be called *les mignardises*, *les petits gâteaux*, *les gourmandises* or *les petites douceurs*. All the names are meant to evoke something sweet and tempting!

▸ A FIRM FAVOURITE WITH FRENCH CHILDREN

COOKING TECHNIQUES

≡ There are numerous technical terms in French cuisine, most of which you will never use or need to understand. However, some techniques are referred to in everyday language when talking about preparing food and it helps to know their meaning. You will also appear really knowledgeable!

≡ Luckily a lot of French terms are widely used in many languages, owing to the predominance and reputation of French cuisine. Consequently you will have no difficulty understanding *mariner* or *une marinade*. Similarly *braiser* and *blanchir* will pose no problem, and you can probably make a good guess for *rôtir*, to roast.

≡ If you need to cook something using *un bain-marie*, you will also recognise the term. Did you know, though, that the word *marie* probably refers to a 16th-century alchemist called Marie-la-Juive? As an alchemist, he would heat base metals in the hope of turning them into gold.

▸ *LE FOIE GRAS POÊLÉ* IS POPULAR AS A STARTER.

LANGUAGE CHECKLIST: COOKING TECHNIQUES

faire revenir to brown
poêler to fry
faire dégorger to add salt and leave to drain
ébouillanter to blanch
cuire à l'étouffée to steam
cuire à la vapeur to steam
mijoter to simmer
le dressage to present attractively

≡ *Faire revenir* doesn't mean, surprisingly, to make something come back, but rather to brown something, usually meat. Alternatively, if you fry the meat, you need to use the verb *poêler*. *Le foie gras poêlé* is a delicacy.

≡ *Faire dégorger* may sound a little violent, as *la gorge* is the throat and *égorger* is to slit someone's throat. However, *faire dégorger* means simply to spread salt on a vegetable, such as cucumbers, in order to drain the water.

≡ *Ébouillanter* means to scald, but when talking about vegetables it simply means to blanch. *Cuire à l'étouffée* also sounds violent, as *étouffer* means to suffocate. However, it simply refers to steaming vegetables. If you prefer you can use *cuire à la vapeur*, which also means to steam.

≡ French cooks will often boast about how long they have left their dish to simmer, *mijoter*. *Mijoter un complot* does not mean to prepare a delicious dish, though, but rather to hatch a plot!

≡ *Le dressage* is the taming or training of an animal. Nowadays, it is also an important factor for contestants in televised cooking competitions. It is the term used for the way the different elements of a dish are placed attractively on the plate before serving. *Un bon dressage* can assure victory!

Describing tastes and textures

≡ French wine lovers have a large vocabulary to describe the characteristics of good wine. Similarly, French people comment knowledgeably about food and its taste and texture. With just a few key words, you can understand what is being said and maybe give your opinion too.

≡ *C'est très bon*, a French person will say when the food is good. If a dish is tasty, you will also hear, *C'est très goûteux* or *Ça a beaucoup de goût*, meaning it's full of flavour.

≡ Positive comments are often about the texture of food. A cake will be *moelleux*, moist; an apple or a salad, *croquant*, crisp; a dessert, *croustillant*, crunchy, or *crémeux*, creamy. When meat is very tender, the French will say, *La viande est fondante*. A melt-in-your-mouth dessert or a luscious fruit will be *fondant* too.

≡ The seasoning of a dish is often a subject of discussion around a dinner table. French people love to debate as to whether the food is a little salty, *un peu salé*, or not salty enough, *pas assez salé*. Ideally the food should be *bien assaisonné*, seasoned just right.

Tous les goûts sont dans la nature means there's no accounting for taste.

You may hear a seemingly dramatic expression about suffocating Christians. It's commonly used to describe food that is stodgy. *C'est un peu étouffe-chrétien.*

≡ Food may be spicy, *épicé*, but don't make the mistake of translating this kind of hot by the word *chaud*. French people won't understand what you mean. Use *très épicé* or *très relevé* instead.

≡ Make sure you don't insult your hostess. *Nourrissant* means nourishing, as you might expect, but it has a negative connotation when used about a meal someone has prepared. It sounds as if you can't find anything more positive to say!

≡ If you find a dessert or a fruitcake rich and use the word *riche*, you will meet blank stares. This concept doesn't really exist in French. However, the French do talk about *la nourriture riche* when referring to a *cuisine* that uses a lot of butter, cream or rich sauces.

≡ If you want to be critical in a restaurant, you can soften the comment by using *un peu*, meaning a little. When you find the meat fatty, the fish overcooked or the endives bitter, you can say, *La viande est un peu grasse. Le poisson est un peu trop cuit. Les endives sont un peu amères.* There's always some comment to make, as talking about food is a national pastime in France!

Food idioms

≡ *Long comme un jour sans pain.* Yes, a day without bread seems endless to a French person. When there's a lot of work to do, that can also be expressed with a bread metaphor. *Il y a du pain sur la planche.* And if somebody isn't worth his salt, *Il ne vaut pas le pain qu'il mange*.

≡ Bread can be associated with good things also. If you buy something for a song, you buy it for *une bouchée de pain*, a mouthful of bread. Somebody who is kind-hearted is *bon comme du bon pain*, and if you think something is worth a try as it doesn't involve much effort, you can say, *Ça ne mange pas de pain*.

≡ Dairy products, even when associated with vegetables, have a positive connotation. When French people say something will add butter to the spinach, *Ça mettra du beurre dans les épinards*, it means it will improve matters. When a drink *se boit comme du petit lait*, it means it's lapped up, and if someone *a fait son beurre*, it means he's made a lot of money.

NO MORE BEANS

The expression *C'est la fin des haricots* probably came to mean a hopeless situation because beans were the staple diet of soldiers and so running out of beans was a disaster.

▸ *J'AI DU PAIN SUR LA PLANCHE !*

Vegetables are often bad news, whether it's the carrots that are cooked, *Les carottes sont cuites*, or when there are no more beans, *C'est la fin des haricots*. Both mean you're done for. When cabbage is evoked, it's a problem also. *Être dans les choux* is to be in a fix. As for turnips, when a film is *un navet*, it's really awful. The director may find afterwards that he is without a radish, *sans un radis*, meaning he's broke.

However, you shouldn't try to have your cake and eat it, *avoir le beurre et l'argent du beurre*, and if you proclaim, *Je ne suis pas une vache à lait !* then you're saying you're not made of money. Hopefully you won't be pedalling in yoghurt, *pédaler dans le yaourt*, as that means you're getting nowhere, and if you are walking on eggs, *marcher sur des œufs*, it means you have to tread carefully in a particular situation.

Don't forget, though, that if someone irritates you too much and you want to tell them to take a running jump, you can always suggest they go and cook an egg, *Va te faire cuire un œuf !*

10 ESSENTIAL VERBS WHEN PREPARING FOOD

≡ The French have numerous words for all the precise techniques and kitchen utensils used when preparing food. However, only experienced cooks will know all the terms involved. Most people will use just a few basic terms when they talk about the various implements and techniques they use.

≡ *Un couteau*, a knife, is, of course, the most common kitchen utensil, and *couper*, to cut, is what you do with a knife. Usually things are cut into pieces, *les morceaux*, or into slices, *les tranches*. If French cooks need to cut vegetables more precisely, then they will dice them, *couper les légumes en dés*. If food needs chopping, then the verb *hacher* will be used.

≡ One of the least appealing tasks when preparing vegetables is peeling them, *éplucher les légumes*. When performing this chore, people will often use the old military expression *Je suis de pluches*. I'm on potato-peeling duty. A potato peeler is *un éplucheur de pommes de terre* or *un économe*.

≡ When making a mayonnaise or a tasty sauce, a whisk, *un fouet*, is used. *Fouetter* is to whisk or to whip. If whisking by hand is too tiring, then cooks can resort to an electric whisk, *un batteur*. When it's a question of beating eggs, then the verb *battre* is used.

If it's simply a question of mixing ingredients, then *mélanger* is used. If you are mixing ingredients for cakes, then you may use *un robot*, which may sound a little frightening but it is, in fact, simply a food processor.

There's an easy verb to remember when making soup. After cooking the vegetables, French cooks will *mixer la soupe* with, not surprisingly, *un mixeur*. The soup will of course be served with the help of *une louche*, a ladle.

When it is necessary to drain food after cooking, *une passoire*, a strainer, is used to drain the vegetables or pasta, *égoutter les pâtes*.

As for desserts, when making pastry French *pâtissiers* will use *un rouleau à pâtisserie* to roll out the pastry, *étaler la pâte*. Before that they will have added all the necessary ingredients.

Ajouter, to add, is of course a key verb to know no matter which dish is being prepared.

LANGUAGE CHECKLIST: ESSENTIAL VERBS

couper to cut
hacher to chop
éplucher to peel
fouetter to whisk/whip
battre to beat
mélanger to mix
mixer to liquidize
égoutter to drain
étaler to roll out
ajouter to add

▸ C'EST VRAIMENT DÉLICIEUX. COMMENT TU FAIS ÇA ?

ASKING QUESTIONS

≡ When talking about food with French people, you will undoubtedly have lots of questions. If an appetising dish is placed before you, you will want to know its name. You can ask, *Comment appelle-t-on ce plat ?*

≡ If you're not quite sure what the dish is, you can ask for an explanation. Remember to pay a compliment first, though, so that your query doesn't appear impolite. You can say, *Ça a l'air délicieux. Qu'est-ce que c'est ?*

≡ When the dish seems to require a certain technique for eating it, or you suspect that there is a particular procedure to be observed, you can ask, *Comment ça se mange ?*

≡ When you've tasted a dish and there's a particular ingredient you can't identify, you can enquire as to what is in the dish. *Qu'est-ce qu'il y a dedans ?* Or you can try and guess and then check to see if you're right. *C'est bien du veau ?* It's veal, isn't it? *Ce sont des panais ?* Are these parsnips?

Mettre les petits plats dans les grands means to to put on a marvellous spread.

En faire tout un plat is to make a song and dance about something.

Mettre les pieds dans le plat is to put one's foot in it.

- Your hosts will be delighted if you enquire about the seasoning, especially if you say that there is a taste you can't quite identify. *Je n'arrive pas à identifier l'assaisonnement. Qu'est-ce que c'est ?* It shows that you are really tasting and appreciating the dish.

- When some ingredients, such as particular spices, are unusual, you can ask where you can find them. *Où est-ce qu'on achète ces épices ?* You may also want to know if you can find them easily. *Ça se trouve facilement ?*

- Of course, there's one question that will really delight your hosts. When you really appreciate a dish, you can ask how it's made, thus giving your hosts the opportunity to shine! *Ça se prépare comment ? Comment vous l'avez fait ?*

- Remember that in France commenting and enquiring about the food you are eating is a sign that you are enjoying the dishes and provides the opportunity for your hosts to talk about what they have prepared. If you don't comment or ask questions and just pay a general compliment at the end, your hosts may well feel that you have not really appreciated their efforts. You may not even be invited again!

Opinions and prejudices

≡ When in France, you will hear French people talking about food a lot. Young and old all have opinions and comment freely on what they are eating or what they like and don't like. If you want to start a conversation around a table, ask a French person what they think about a dish, *Qu'est-ce que vous en pensez ?* You will receive a full and usually well-informed reply.

≡ When they like a dish, French people will say, *C'est très bon.* In an informal context, you will hear people say, *C'est super bon ! C'est extra ! C'est génial !* They will then elaborate on the reasons for this positive opinion.

When a French person doesn't like something served in a restaurant, he will say, *Ce n'est pas super. Ce n'est pas très bon.* If a higher standard was expected, he will express his disappointment, *Je suis déçu*.

French restaurants do not cater particularly for vegetarians, although increasingly there will be at least one dish on the menu that is without meat or fish. Generally, French people express surprise that someone can exist on a vegetarian diet and also incomprehension that anyone could choose to give up so many good things. *Que c'est bizarre !*

FOOD FACTS

More pizzas are eaten in France than in Italy.

More hamburgers are eaten in France than in any other European country, except for Britain.

35,000 tons of snails are eaten in France every year.

More wine is drunk per inhabitant in France than in any other country in the world.

The French often have a negative image of British food. They relate tales of school exchanges where they remember eating jelly, meat boiled in water, overcooked vegetables and peas with mint. *Quelle horreur !* There is even a cooking technique called *cuire à l'anglaise*, which is used when something is boiled in salted water, although in France it's usually vegetables.

Le fast-food is similarly frowned upon. Spending time around a table discussing and eating good food is one of life's great pleasures for French people. The French do have expressions for a quick snack, *manger sur le pouce*, literally to eat on one's thumb, but it's only when there is no alternative.

Les produits de terroir are the products that are the most respected in France. These are local products seen to have an *authenticité* and are part of the traditions of a specific region, grown in a specific soil or produced in a time-honoured manner. They are often ingredients in regional recipes and help to create a regional identity.

QUIZ

1. **Match the first half of the sentence with its second half.**

a. *Je le préfère*	**1.** *gâteau au chocolat.*
b. *Je ne mange pas*	**2.** *babas au rhum.*
c. *Je voudrais un*	**3.** *saignant, s'il vous plaît.*
d. *J'adore les*	**4.** *de pain.*

2. **Place the courses in the right order.**

a. *les mignardises*
b. *le dessert*
c. *l'entrée*
d. *les amuse-bouches*
e. *le plat principal*
f. *le fromage*

3. **Match the English word with its French equivalent.**

a. *hacher*	**1.** to simmer
b. *poêler*	**2.** to brown
c. *mijoter*	**3.** to chop
d. *éplucher*	**4.** to fry
e. *faire revenir*	**5.** to peel

Solutions on page 96.

DISHES TO DISCOVER

LITERARY DISHES

Probably the best-known reference to food in French literature is in Proust's DU CÔTÉ DE CHEZ SWANN, when a series of recollections are triggered by the narrator eating *une madeleine*. These small, shell-shaped cakes, made in Commercy, in the east of France, were supposedly created by a peasant girl called Madeleine.

Simenon, creator of the famous Commissaire Maigret, frequently mentioned authentic Parisian cafés in his novels with specific references to the dishes his hero ate. In MAIGRET ET LA JEUNE MORTE, Maigret enjoys a traditional onion soup, *une soupe à l'oignon*.

Jacques Prévert memorably starts his poem DÉJEUNER DU MATIN with a description of someone drinking *un café crème*. He lists the steps of a man pouring the coffee, adding milk and then sugar and stirring the coffee before drinking it. The successive gestures gradually reveal the man's total indifference to the other person present.

EAT YOUR WORDS!

Many French verbs having to do with food can also be used when talking about literature. *Se nourrir de la littérature, savourer une histoire, goûter un livre* and even *faire une indigestion de mots !*

▸ MAIGRET ENJOYED A TRADITIONAL ONION SOUP.

≡ In MADAME BOVARY, Flaubert describes an elaborate French wedding cake, *une pièce montée*, in minute detail. It is very different from a modern *pièce montée*, which is made of caramelised balls of choux pastry filled with confectioner's custard and piled high on top of each other in a pyramid shape.

≡ In Zola's L'ASSOMMOIR, the sensual description of a roast goose, *une oie rôtie*, as it is placed on the table and then carved and eaten by the guests becomes a metaphor for the body of the young Gervaise, who serves it.

≡ Colette's recipe for *le vin d'oranges* is lovingly detailed in PRISONS ET PARADIS. The heady mixture involving four litres of wine and a litre of Armagnac, as well as Provençal oranges, a lemon, a vanilla pod and cane sugar, is made into a winter elixir to cure all ills!

≡ In Rostand's CYRANO DE BERGERAC, the character Ragueneau famously gives instructions for making almond tartlets, *les tartelettes amandines*. The tartlets are still made today following Ragueneau's recipe. They are notably served in Le Ragueneau, a restaurant and tearoom, *un salon de thé*, in Paris.

≡ *Une blanquette de veau* is the source of a debate between a young girl's grandparents in Henri Troyat's novel VIOU. The eight-year-old girl tries to become part of the adult world by joining in the argument. Classic dishes continue to provoke animated discussions around the dining table.

Amusing Dishes

≡ Potatoes in dressing gowns? This may sound a surprising way of eating potatoes. In fact *les pommes de terre en robe de chambre* refers to baked or jacket potatoes. The term is sometimes spelled *robe des champs*, literally meaning the dress of the fields.

≡ If you eat *un financier*, you are not eating a financial specialist but rather a cake made of ground almonds, *les amandes pilées*. The cake, shaped like a gold bar, *un lingot*, was the idea of a Parisian *pâtissier* in the late 19th century. His shop was near the Stock Exchange, *la Bourse*.

≡ You can also eat *une religieuse*, a nun. This is a cake made from two balls of choux pastry, *la pâte à choux*, and filled with confectioner's custard, *la crème pâtissière*. The smaller ball, placed on top of the other, represents the head, and the two are coated with chocolate. The result resembles a rather rotund friar. The cake is always feminine however.

> *Donner sa langue au chat* is to give up when playing a game or during a competition.

≡ When you go to someone's house, you may be invited to sit on the sofa, *le canapé*. Your hosts may also offer you *des canapés* to eat. These are open sandwiches frequently served with *un apéritif* drink.

≡ *Le tablier de sapeur* literally means a sapper's or a soldier's apron. Even some French people might wonder what this is when they see it on a menu. It's a speciality made of tripe, *le gras-double*, and owes its name to the leather aprons worn by sappers, the soldiers who dig and repair fortifications. It is served in Lyon's traditional restaurants, known as *les bouchons*.

When a French person talks about *le pain perdu*, they are not referring to a loaf they have lost. Slices of slightly stale bread, *du pain rassis*, soaked in milk, coated in beaten eggs and fried in butter and then sugared make a dessert that reminds many French children of their childhood.

Le Paris-Brest is a cake named after the Paris-Brest bicycle race. It is made from choux pastry and filled with a praline-flavoured cream, *une crème mousseline pralinée*. It was created to celebrate the famous race, and its circular shape represents a bicycle wheel.

If someone offers you *une langue-de-chat*, a cat's tongue, don't be horrified: it's simply a finger biscuit that is very popular in France.

Violent dishes

Some French dishes have violent names. *Une bombe glacée* is a dome-shaped ice-cream pudding. It has nothing to do with bombs, as it was intended to resemble a cannonball. It has been a popular French dessert since the end of the 19th century.

Le canard au sang sounds like a really bloodthirsty dish. It is made with ducks from the Rouen area in the north of France. After being partially cooked, the breasts, *les blancs*, and the legs, *les cuisses*, are removed, and the remaining meat, carcass and skin is put through a press to extract the blood, *le sang*, and juices. This mixture is then seasoned and added to the breasts to finish cooking. The legs are served as a separate course afterwards, usually with a salad. The dish was made famous by the Tour d'Argent restaurant in Paris in the mid-19th century.

Ça ne casse pas trois pattes à un canard means it's nothing to write home about.

If you see *la cervelle de canut* on a restaurant menu, you may think it is a dish made from brains, *la cervelle*. However, it is a cheese dish made from drained milk curds, *le fromage blanc*, beaten and seasoned with garlic, chives, parsley and salt and pepper. *Les canuts* were the traditional silk workers in Lyon.

Les poires tapées, or beaten pears, are a speciality of Rivarennes near Tours. This traditional method for conserving fruit was revived in the 1980s. The pears are peeled and then dehydrated in special ovens and finally flattened to remove all the air. No colouring, sugar or preservatives are added, and the pears can be kept for several years.

Les carottes à l'étouffée has nothing to do with suffocating carrots, despite the fact that *étouffer* means to suffocate. It is simply the term for steaming vegetables, *cuire à l'étouffée*.

Frapper means to hit, but of course *le champagne frappé* means simply champagne that is chilled. The expression comes from the mixture of water and ice-cubes used to chill the champagne, which is ideally served at a temperature of around 6°C. The term *frappé* comes from the ice-cubes knocking against the bottle of champagne as they float in the water. Nowadays *le champagne frappé* can also mean iced champagne, when the champagne is placed in a bucket of ice. This is not recommended by specialists.

Dishes for towns

Every town in France seems to have its culinary speciality, and some more than one! Cakes, cheeses and *charcuterie* products are, unsurprisingly, the most frequently cited as being distinctive.

Cheeses named after towns, such as *le brie de Meaux*, *le munster* or *le camembert*, are numerous. There are goat's cheeses such as *le cabécou de Rocamadour*, produced since the 15th century, and blue cheeses such as *le Roquefort*, known since the 11th century.

La fourme d'Ambert is a large, circular blue cheese dating from Roman times, possibly even earlier. Its name comes from the Latin 'forma', which is probably the origin of the word *fromage*.

The *charcuterie* products of one town are often considered by the inhabitants to be superior to those of another. *Les saucisses de Strasbourg* are different from *les saucisses de Toulouse* and different again from *la saucisse de Morteau*. *Les andouillettes de Troyes* are renowned, as are *les rillettes du Mans*.

En faire tout un fromage is to make a song and dance about something.

La remarque ne manque pas de sel means it's quite a witty remark.

≡ *Le jambon de Bayonne* is one of the most famous *charcuterie* products. Legend has it that a boar fell into salty water and was discovered, well conserved, a year later. It is said that it is the quality of this local salt, used to conserve *le jambon de Bayonne*, which makes this ham so special.

≡ Many towns claim to have a special cake or sweet specialities. In addition to *les madeleines de Commercy*, made famous by Proust, there are also *les galettes de Pont-Aven*, *les macarons de Nancy*, *les calissons d'Aix-en-Provence* and le *nougat de Montélimar*.

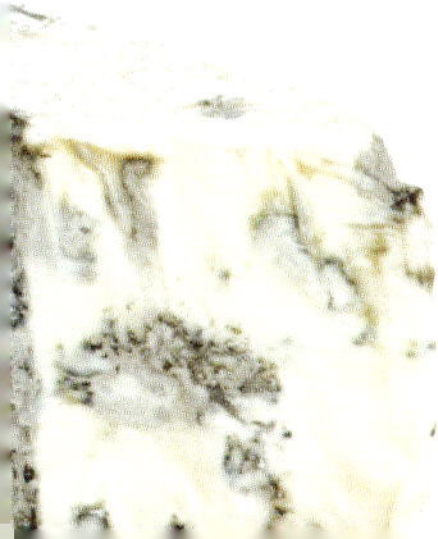

≡ *Le canaule* was originally a type of bread made with egg yolks. A *pâtissier* in Bordeaux reinvented it as a small cake and added rum and vanilla. As the original name resembled the word *cannelé*, meaning fluted, he cooked them in individual fluted moulds. *Les cannelés de Bordeaux* can be eaten as snacks, for breakfast or as a dessert.

≡ Numerous other towns have specialities. There's *le pruneau d'Agen*, *le melon de Cavaillon*, *la lentille verte du Puy*, *les tripes de Caen*, *la moutarde de Dijon* and the famous *salade niçoise*. Every town in France seems to consider that, if it doesn't have a gastronomic speciality, it is not worth its salt. That would be a special salt, of course: *le sel de Guérande!*

Famous Name Dishes

Le tournedos Henri IV is a classic French dish of beef fillet, *le filet de bœuf*, accompanied by *la sauce béarnaise*. It was invented in the 1830s in Le Pavillon Henri IV, a restaurant near Paris named after this much-loved king who ruled France between 1589 and 1610.

The king, who enjoyed good food, came from the region of Béarn and was known as *le grand Béarnais*. The sauce was an invention of the restaurant's chef who, having spoilt the sauce he was making, adapted it, thus creating one of the great classic French sauces.

When Paul Bocuse was awarded *la Legion d'honneur* in 1975, the French President, Valéry Giscard d'Estaing, gave a meal in his honour at le Palais de l'Elysée. The great French chef was asked to create *l'entrée*. He presented a truffle soup, in individual dishes, with a pastry crust. The dish became known as *la soupe aux truffes noires de VGE*, the president's initials. It remains on the menu of Bocuse's restaurant in Collonges-au-Mont-d'Or today.

Le chateaubriand is a recipe based on a cut of tenderloin steak between two and four centimetres thick. The name refers to the way the meat is cooked rather then the cut itself. Montmireil, chef to the famous writer and

▸ THE FAMOUS *SAUCE BÉARNAISE*

diplomat François-René de Chateaubriand, probably created the dish in 1822, and it may even have been served for the first time in the French Embassy in London, although there is no historical proof.

Allonger la sauce is to pad things out.

À quelle sauce allons-nous être mangés ? means 'I wonder what fate has in store for us.'

≡ *La charlotte* is named after Queen Charlotte, the wife of King George III. It was a popular bread-and-butter pudding served hot. Carême, the most famous French *pâtissier* of his time, saw the dessert when working in London for the Prince Regent, the future George IV.

≡ Later, when working for Talleyrand, Carême invented *les boudoirs* or *les biscuits à la cuillère*, sponge fingers. Around 1800, he used *les boudoirs* in an adaptation of the English recipe, placing them around the sides of a high mould and filling the centre with Bavarian cream, *la crème bavaroise*. He called the dessert *une charlotte à la parisienne*. When he worked for the Czar Alexander, he renamed it *une charlotte à la russe*, which later became *une charlotte russe* as it is known today.

Surprises in your dish

≡ You will frequently see items on French menus that pique your curiosity. It may be an unusual combination, or simply a name that intrigues. Or sometimes you may be served a dish with an unexpected ingredient, or with an astonishing presentation. French chefs like to surprise!

≡ If you find *un café gourmand* on your dessert menu, you may well wonder what it is. You will probably have tasted a *café liégeois*, made of coffee, ice-cream and whipped cream, but *un café gourmand* is a more recent trend. The idea is simple: a small cup of black coffee and small portions of different desserts, usually including a rich chocolate dessert. The presentation is visually attractive with different shapes and colours, and the opportunity to try several desserts at once makes it a truly *gourmand* experience.

≡ Everybody recognises *les mille-feuilles*, those delicious vanilla slices made of layers of puff pastry and confectioner's custard. You may, however, find an apparent *mille-feuille* as your starter or as part of your main course. Savoury food, when assembled to look like a dessert, brings the visual attractiveness and creativity that often characterise cakes, as well as interesting combinations of different textures. It's a pleasing association.

≡ Flowers can be colourful additions to some dishes. They are not just for decoration either! You can try their surprising textures and flavours in salads or as accompaniments to a main course. Some French chefs have made flowers part of their signature dishes, and in a few daring restaurants, the menu is dedicated to dishes with flowers as a principal ingredient.

▸ A LITTLE BIT OF EVERYTHING, PLUS A COFFEE!

≡ Things are not always what they seem when French cooks decide to innovate. To surprise the taste buds, what looks like rice may turn out to be carefully diced and shaped pieces of squid. The contrast between the visual impression and the nature and texture of the food is intended to ensure that real attention is given to taste.

≡ Alongside the tradition of classic French cuisine, French chefs like to incorporate unfamiliar ingredients that bring new tastes and flavours. These can be vegetables or fruit that have not been cultivated for generations or spices and vegetables from other continents. Following the recent influences of Asian cuisines, attention is now being paid to African food. French chefs will continue to surprise!

DEATH OF THE *JAMBON-BEURRE?*

Is the iconic ham sandwich in a baguette on its way out? Even more surprisingly, is it being replaced by burgers? In 2000, one burger was sold for every nine traditional sandwiches, but in 2013, one burger was sold for every two sandwiches.

Seasonal French Dishes

≡ The French love celebrating the changes in the seasons and make sure they take advantage of the times when it is best to eat certain foods. The arrival of *le Beaujolais nouveau* on the third Thursday of November is not the only thing noted on French culinary calendars!

≡ It has long been a tradition in France to consider the appearance of asparagus on market stalls as a sign of the arrival of spring. Bundles of both green and the thicker white asparagus abound for a few weeks in April and early May. Asparagus are usually steamed and eaten with French dressing, *une vinaigrette*, or *une sauce hollandaise*.

Se fermer comme une huître means to clam up.

Appuyer sur le champignon means to put one's foot down when driving.

Un chapeau melon is a bowler hat.

≡ Summer sees melons arriving on market stalls and on restaurant menus. *Les melons de Cavaillon*, a town in sun-drenched Provence, are just one of the varieties that are popular. Sliced and married with paper-thin slices of *un jambon de Bayonne* or, for smaller melons, halved and hollowed out and filled with a muscatel or port wine, they are a refreshing and simple *entrée* for meals taken outside.

Le saucisson au gêne is prepared with the pulp of grapes once they have been pressed. It is therefore typically a dish popular in the autumn as the grape-harvesting period comes to an end. Thick sausages, *les saucisses à cuire*, are cooked with the grape marc and a liberal amount of red wine. In the Beaujolais, this dish is often the centrepiece of a communal festive meal enjoyed by the village residents.

Autumn is also heralded by the appearance on market stalls of several varieties of mushrooms and, in southwest France, sellers along the roadsides selling the prized *cèpes* mushrooms. The latter are expensive but, sliced and tossed in butter, their distinctive taste transforms a simple meal into a feast.

Tradition maintained that oysters, *les huîtres*, should only be eaten during months with an 'r' in the name. It was seen as unwise to eat oysters during the summer months. With improvements in refrigerated transport, this is no longer true, but French people still see the tempting displays of oysters outside *brasseries* in the winter as a welcome sign of the approaching festive season.

Asking for dishes

In order to discover new dishes when in France, you need to be able to ask for them. Every French region has its specialities, so you can simply say in a restaurant, *Je voudrais un plat typique de la région*. Or, *Je voudrais une spécialité locale, s'il vous plaît.* When you want to be really polite, you can say, *J'aimerais goûter un plat typique d'ici, s'il vous plaît.*

You can also inquire which dishes on the menu are local specialities by asking, *Qu'est-ce que vous avez comme plat régional ?* Or you could ask, *Est-ce que vous avez une spécialité locale ?*

If there is an item on the menu that you don't know, you can ask, *C'est un plat typique d'ici ?* Or, *Est-ce que c'est une spécialité régionale ?*

When you want further explanations, you can ask how the dish is prepared, *Comment est-ce que ce plat est préparé ?* You can also ask what it contains, *Qu'est-ce qu'il y a dedans ?* Or, *Quels sont les ingrédients ?*

If you would like to know more about the traditions concerning the dish, you can ask, *Quel est l'origine de ce plat ?* Or, *Comment ça se prépare traditionnellement ?*

Some local dishes may have names that are difficult to pronounce. A popular dessert in Brittany, for example, is *le kouign-amann*. You can always ask for help, *Comment ça se prononce ?* Or, *Ca se dit comment ?* When the name seems unusual, you may want to know the origin of the dish's name. *C'est du breton ?* Is that Breton? *C'est du provençal ?* Is that Provençal?

▸ *LE KOUIGN-AMANN* IS A GOOD CHOICE FOR DESSERT IF YOU KNOW HOW TO PRONOUNCE IT!

≡ If you go into a delicatessen, *une épicerie fine*, or *une charcuterie traiteur*, you can discover the name of something you see by pointing to it and asking, *Comment ça s'appelle ?* You can then check that it is a local speciality, *C'est fait par ici ?* Or, *C'est une spécialité locale ?*

≡ If you want to know more, you can ask, *Qu'est-ce que c'est exactement ?* If it has a particular shape or colour, you can inquire, *La forme est traditionnelle ? Ça a toujours cette couleur ?* In answer to your questions you will almost certainly be told, at some point, *C'est très bon !*

LANGUAGE CHECKLIST: REQUESTS

Je voudrais... I'd like...
J'aimerais goûter... I'd like to try...
Est-ce que vous avez...? Do you have...?
Comment ça se prépare ? How is it prepared?
Comment ça se prononce ? How do you pronounce it?
Comment ça s'appelle ? What's that called?

QUIZ

1. Match the name of the dish with the town.

a. *Les saucisses de*	1. *Caen*
b. *Le brie de*	2. *Montélimar*
c. *Le jambon de*	3. *Strasbourg*
d. *Le nougat de*	4. *Meaux*
e. *Les tripes de*	5. *Bayonne*

2. Circle the odd man out.

a. *un Paris-Brest*	*un financier*	*une religieuse*	*une langue-de-chat*
b. *les huîtres*	*les moules*	*les asperges*	*les escargots*
c. *une charlotte*	*le pain perdu*	*un chateaubriand*	*la sauce béarnaise*
d. *un café crème*	*un café liégeois*	*une mousse au café*	*un café gourmand*

3. Fill in the blanks using the words below.
comment, dedans, ingrédients, typique, spécialité

a. *Vous avez une ____________ locale ?*
b. *J'aimerais goûter un plat _________.*
c. *__________ ça se prononce ?*
d. *Qu'est-ce qu'il y a __________ ?*
e. *Quels sont les __________ ?*

Solutions on page 96.

GOOD THINGS TO KNOW

SETTING THE TABLE

When French people lay the table, they say they are going to *dresser la table* or *mettre la table*. As spending time together eating a meal is important, the table will be set quite formally, especially when there are guests or for a family gathering.

The table is covered with a tablecloth, *une nappe*, and the dishes, *les assiettes*, and the glasses, *les verres*, are added. There are wineglasses, *les verres à vin*, and water glasses, *les verres à eau*. A napkin, *une serviette de table*, is put by each place setting.

Le gîte et le couvert means board and lodgings.

Il n'y va pas avec le dos de la cuillère means he doesn't do anything halfway.

Être à couteaux tirés is to be at daggers drawn.

The cutlery or flatware, *les couverts*, consisting of a fork, *une fourchette*, a knife, *un couteau*, and a dessert spoon, *une cuillère à dessert*, are placed as well. If there is soup, as is often the case for the family evening meal, *une cuillère à soupe* is added. The expression *mettre le couvert* can also be used to mean laying the table.

▸ S'ASSURER QUE TOUT EST EN PLACE

≡ In some families, the forks are placed with the tips of the prongs touching the table and the rounded back of the fork in the air. In the past, this was to make sure the guests saw the silver hallmark stamped on the fork.

≡ Small plates for the starter, *l'entrée*, are usually placed on top of the dinner plates. They are then removed before the main course. After the main course, small plates and knives are brought for the cheese. Finally, *les assiettes à dessert* are used for the dessert course.

≡ There are no side plates for bread, which is served in a breadbasket. Each person will then take a piece and place it on the tablecloth next to his or her plate.

≡ There are also table mats, *les dessous-de-plat*, for the serving dishes, *les plats de service*, and serving spoons, *les cuillères de service*. If there is sauce with the main dish, this is served in *une saucière*.

≡ There may also be coasters, *les dessous-de-verre*, and *un dessous-de-bouteille* for placing under the bottle of wine.

≡ When the meal is finished, the family members will help to clear the table, *débarrasser la table*. Coffee, in small cups, *les tasses à café*, is usually served in the living room.

TABLE MANNERS

≡ Table manners in France are generally the same as in most countries. However, some customs differ and it is best to follow the French tradition rather than risk surprising or even shocking your host.

≡ Your hostess will invite you to the table by saying, *À table !* or, more formally, *Si vous voulez bien passer à table*.

≡ In France, it is common to organise the seating around the table so that women and men alternate. In some family gatherings, the eldest son is seated next to his mother, and the daughter, or alternatively the eldest son's wife, is seated next to the father. Not all families respect this rule, but it is important to wait for your hostess to seat you.

- The service plate is passed first to the person on the host's right. Sometimes, in a more informal gathering, the hostess will serve each guest herself. She will suggest this by saying, *Je vais vous servir*, or, *Je vous sers ?* It is polite to accept by replying, *Merci, c'est gentil*.

- Use a knife and fork to eat, rather than just a fork on its own, and keep the fork in the left hand. When pausing during eating, you can rest the knife and fork on each side of the plate with the handles resting on the table. In a restaurant, if you place the knife and fork completely on the plate, this can be understood as a sign that you have finished eating.

- Your hands should always remain in sight when not eating. You can place your wrists on the edge of the table.

- When eating bread, you should break off a small piece and eat it rather than biting into a larger piece.

- When eating soup, you are not expected to tip your plate away from you or to sip from the side of the spoon as in some countries.

PATIENCE IS EXPECTED

French children become used to long French meals from an early age. They are told to behave well, *Tiens-toi bien à table !* If the meal is very long, the children may be given permission to leave the table, *Tu peux sortir de table*.

- Your water glass will be the largest of the glasses placed in front of you. You will also have one or two glasses for white and red wine, depending on the formality of the occasion. If you do not wish your glass to be refilled, you can simply place your open hand, palm down, a little above your glass and say, *Non merci*.

How to eat certain dishes

≡ What is the polite way to eat unfamiliar food? You can simply copy your French neighbour at the table, but it is useful to know a few basic techniques.

≡ Artichokes can be a little daunting. Most French people place an upturned fork or spoon under their plate to hold it at an angle. They then put the sauce accompanying the artichoke in the lower part of the plate, allowing them, as they pick off the leaves, to dip them in the sauce before drawing the leaf across the lower teeth to obtain the flesh. The leaves are then piled on the plate or in a separate dish. The tips of the smaller leaves near the centre are eaten together. The choke is then carefully removed, and the artichoke base is cut up with a knife and fork and dipped in the sauce.

≡ Asparagus can be eaten with the fingers or a knife and fork, depending on the recipe. They are usually eaten dipped in a sauce. It's best to start with the tender tip. If, near the base of the asparagus, it becomes a little woody, you can leave this part.

To finish any sauce on your plate, you should place a piece of bread on the prongs of your fork to soak up the sauce. In informal gatherings, though, people usually hold the bread with their fingers.

It is considered extremely polite to eat any fruit served whole with a knife and fork. Try peeling a peach, however, with your knife and fork and you will see that it's only for experts!

If you want to try eating snails, you will be given a special fork. Simply remove the snail from its shell and place it whole in your mouth. It's really the sauce that has been placed in the shell that makes snails such a tasty morsel.

When served frog's legs, you will need to use your fingers. Simply suck the delicate flesh off the bones. You will be given a fingerbowl or lemon towel to remove the sauce from your fingers afterwards.

If, after eating some of these garlic-rich dishes, you worry about your breath smelling, copy the French and chew a sprig of fresh parsley or a few grains of ground coffee!

▸ *UNE PETITE CUISSE DE GRENOUILLE ?*

VALUE FOR MONEY!

The French comedian Coluche joked that artichokes were a dish for the poor, as there seems to be more on the plate after eating than at the beginning. *« C'est le seul plat que quand t'as fini de manger, t'en as plus dans ton assiette que quand t'as commencé ! »*

The French and food

≡ Food is respected in France, and eating habits have not changed radically in recent years. French people continue to eat three meals a day: in the morning, at midday and in the evening. There is little snacking in between, with the exception of *le goûter*, a teatime snack for young children after school.

≡ The midday and evening meals are eaten at fixed times across France. Recent studies have shown that, at 1pm, half the nation is eating lunch. In provincial French towns, traffic becomes busy around midday as people return home for lunch. Motorways have less traffic, as people interrupt their journeys to eat.

≡ The evening meal is generally eaten around 8pm. It is a time when the family meet to discuss their day and spend time together. Only very young children eat separately.

≡ The French spend time over their meals, on average, two hours and 22 minutes per day. That's even longer than a couple of decades ago! Time is also spent preparing food, as meals are considered moments of pleasure in the daily routine.

≡ The French pay attention to their food when eating. Even though the time spent over lunch is generally shorter than it used to be, most people take a break rather than eating at their desk.

≡ The typical French meal is traditionally a starter, main course and dessert.

LIVING TO EAT

In a recent study, a group of Americans were asked what they associated with certain words. For 'chocolate cake', they replied, "Guilt." Given the same word, a French group replied, "Birthday."

However, this is changing a little. Shorter lunch breaks mean many restaurants now propose two-course as well as three-course meals. However, when invited to somebody's home, expect at least three courses.

≡ The French are not always open to individual preferences when it comes to food. It is expected that guests will eat the food the hosts have prepared. They will not be asked in advance if they have special needs. Someone who is vegetarian or who doesn't eat cheese or a particular meat, for example, will feel obliged to explain. Meals are very much a collective experience in France.

≡ French people value time spent sharing a meal with family or friends. Meals are not only key moments during the day but also highlights of leisure time and weekends. In the French culture, food is strongly linked with conviviality. And, of course, around the table, one of the main topics will be food!

Reading Menus

≡ When given a menu in France, you will first need to choose between the set menus, *les menus fixes*, and the *à la carte* section where you can select individual dishes. In very chic restaurants, prices will only appear on the menu given to the person who made the dinner reservation.

≡ There is usually a choice between two or three dishes for each course on set menus. The first menu is the least expensive. It is often called *le menu du marché* or *le menu touristique*. This menu is usually only served at lunchtime.

≡ The highest-priced menu is sometimes called *le menu de dégustation* or *le menu découverte*. It usually highlights *les produits de terroir*, prized local ingredients, or the chef's signature dishes.

≡ On lower-priced menus, instead of the traditional cheese course being followed by dessert, cheese may only be an option instead of a dessert.

FRENCH DRESSING

In the 18th century, it was fashionable in London high society to call upon the services of Chevalier d'Albignac, a French émigré, to season salads. He would go from house to house with the ingredients for *une vinaigrette*, which consequently became known as French dressing in England.

▸ ALORS, QU'EST-CE QUE NOUS ALLONS MANGER CE MIDI ?

≡ On the *à la carte* menu, the dishes for the main course will be classed as *poissons* (fish), *fruits de mer* (seafood), *volaille* (poultry), *viandes* (meat dishes) or, during the season, *gibier* (game).

≡ The name of the dish will usually indicate the cooking method, the accompaniment or whether the main ingredient comes from a particular region. The way the dish has been prepared is usually expressed by using *à la*, *au* or *aux*, as in *à la française*, or *au beurre blanc* or *à l'ancienne* when it is a traditional recipe. An important ingredient can also be highlighted in this way, as in *aux morilles*.

≡ Some elaborate dishes may only be served when ordered by two people at the table. This is indicated on the menu by the words *deux personnes* or *deux convives* in parentheses after the item.

≡ If you have difficulty understanding an item on the menu, you can always request help by asking, *Qu'est-ce que c'est ?* or, *Vous pouvez m'expliquer ce que c'est, s'il vous plaît ?* When it is a particular word that you don't understand, you can ask, *Qu'est-ce que ça veut dire ?*

≡ Nowadays, French menus usually include service charges and taxes. You are not obliged to leave a tip, although you can if you have particularly enjoyed the meal and appreciated the service. There is no rule as to the amount, but 1€ for every 20€ is a fair guideline for most restaurants.

Choosing Wine

≡ On the wine menu, *la carte des vins*, you can choose between white wine, *le vin blanc*, rosé wine, *le vin rosé*, and red wine, *le vin rouge*, or order different wines for specific courses. Throughout your meal, always move from lighter to more powerful and higher-quality wines and never the opposite.

≡ If you're not sure which wine is the best choice, ask the wine waiter, *le sommelier*, *Qu'est-ce que vous suggériez comme vin ?* or, *Quel vin ira le mieux avec le canard ?*

≡ You can choose a full bottle, *une bouteille*, (75cl) or a half bottle, *une demi-bouteille*, (37.5cl). However, the choice of wines in half bottles is often limited. Some restaurants, but not all, serve wine by the glass. If you want the house wine, you can ask for *le vin de la maison*, *un vin de table* or *une carafe de rouge*.

≡ White or rosé wine will be served chilled in an ice bucket, *un seau à glace* or *un seau à rafraîchir*. Red wine will have been brought to room temperature, *chambré*, before serving.

≡ If you choose fish for a starter or main course, it is usual to order white wine. However, many people now order red wine with fish too. In this case, it's important to choose a light red wine, such as *un pinot noir*, or a mature wine that will not overpower the delicate taste of the fish.

For a meat dish, the choice of a red wine will depend a lot on personal taste. However, for red meats, meats with rich sauces and for game, select a wine with a lot of tannin, such as Loire Valley wines or Bordeaux wines. Wines should bring out the best in the dish and vice versa; the taste of the one shouldn't overpower the taste of the other.

Traditionally people drink red wine with cheese, although many experts suggest that most cheeses are best with white wine.

It is a good idea to choose a local wine, *un vin de la région*. There will usually be a good selection on the menu, and this may give you the chance to discover less familiar wines. When eating a local dish, this will also be a natural association. Try a Burgundy wine with *un bœuf bourguignon*.

Mettre de l'eau dans son vin means to make concessions.

Être entre deux vins means to be tipsy.

Cuver son vin means to sleep it off.

Chocolate, a French passion

The French love chocolate. Just before Christmas, Easter, Mother's Day and Valentine's Day, there are queues outside specialised chocolate shops, *les chocolateries*. Each shop will have a large selection of high-quality chocolates, handmade by an expert, *un maître chocolatier*.

On display there will be several boxes, *les ballotins*, of different sizes, each priced according to the weight of chocolate they contain when filled. French people choose the size of the box they require and then make their selection from among the chocolates displayed by pointing. Once full, the box is then tied with pretty ribbons.

≡ On the Thursday before Easter, the church bells in France are silenced. It is said they have gone to Rome. On their return, they drop chocolate-shaped bells, *les cloches au chocolat*, and chocolate eggs, *les œufs de Pâques*, into gardens for children to find.

≡ Chocolates make an excellent gift if you are invited to someone's house in France, or as a thank you. As good French chocolates are expensive, even a small box is appreciated.

≡ Generally, French people eat mainly dark chocolate that is not too sweet. They favour rich chocolate fillings made with butter and cream, *la ganache*, or praline-filled chocolates, *les chocolats pralinés*. Some chocolates will even be decorated with gold leaf, *une feuille d'or*.

≡ A hot chocolate drink, *un chocolat chaud*, is just the thing after a walk on a brisk winter day. Good cafés will pride themselves on the quality of their hot chocolate, and it is a popular choice in France's pavement cafés.

LANGUAGE CHECKLIST: CHOCOLATE

un ballotin a small box (for chocolates)
le chocolat au lait milk chocolate
le chocolat noir dark chocolate
le chocolat blanc white chocolate
la ganache filling made from chocolate, butter and cream
le pralin praline

≡ Chocolate is very much present in cakes and desserts too. French *pâtissiers* give chocolate cakes, such as *un opéra* or *un éclair au chocolat*, pride of place in their displays, and dessert menus in restaurants always include delights such as *un moelleux au chocolat* or hot chocolate sauces. Young children love *les pains au chocolat* for breakfast or as after-school treats too.

≡ One of the disciplines of the esteemed and very difficult competition to become *un meilleur ouvrier de France* is chocolate making. Participants have to make elaborate chocolate sculptures in a given time limit. You can often see similar amazing sculptures in the windows of the most famous *chocolateries*.

Food festivals

≡ As well as enjoying good food when eating out in France, you can also discover gastronomic treats by visiting the many food festivals held throughout France. These vary from annual markets to celebrations of regional specialities.

≡ *Le piment d'Espelette* is honoured the last weekend in October in the village of Espelette in the Basque region. Producers display the brightly coloured peppers, there is traditional Basque music, and in the village restaurants you can savour dishes based on this local speciality. You can also attend a mass in the Basque language during which the peppers are blessed.

≡ On the first Friday in August, the village of Lautrec, in the Tarn, celebrates its famous garlic, *l'ail rose de Lautrec*. There are competitions and parades throughout the day, a colourful market and an outdoor evening meal that starts with a huge garlic soup. The evening is spent dancing in the streets.

≡ *La fête du cassoulet* in Castelnaudary takes place on the last weekend of August. *Le cassoulet* is, of course, the star of the event, but there are also a gourmet food market, samplings of food and wine and nautical events on the nearby Canal du Midi. It's the ideal moment to discover and taste an authentic *cassoulet*.

Faire l'andouille means to act the fool.

Donner du piment à une situation is to add spice to a situation.

≡ If you're touring Brittany, don't miss *La fête de l'andouille* in the small town of Guémenée-sur-Scorff on the second Sunday in August. *L'andouille*, chitterlings sausage, is the local speciality. You can explore the distinctive Breton culture while making your gastronomic discoveries.

≡ Limoges may be known worldwide for its porcelain, but its butchers also have a claim to fame. The historic rue de la Boucherie hosts, on the third Friday of October, *La frairie des petits ventres*. Discover regional dishes on the stalls that line the street as well as sausages, hams and traditional *pâtisseries*. *Le petit ventre* refers to Notre-Dame-des-Petits-Ventres, a statue of the Virgin Mary that is paraded through the streets. It is also a speciality dish of tripe.

≡ Winter fairs have been regular events in Brive-la-Gaillarde since the 13th century. Called *Les foires grasses*, there are four or five between December and March. Producers of *foie gras* come to sell their products as well as their geese and ducks. Prizes are given for the best products on this very French occasion.

QUIZ

1. Are the following statements true or false?

a. In France, you should keep your hands on your lap when not eating.

b. French people generally keep their fork in their left hand.

c. Placing your knife and fork completely on the plate is a sign your have finished eating.

d. Traditionally, the serving dish is passed first to the most important guest.

2. Fill in the missing letters to complete the words.

a. *la v _ _ _ ille* c. *la ser _ _ _ tte*

b. *la cuil _ _ _ _* d. *le g _ _ ier*

3. Fill in the blanks using the verbs below.
expliquer, aller, servir, manger, débarrasser

a. *Je vais __________ la table .*

b. *Vous pouvez m'_________ ce qu c'est ?*

c. *Je vais __________ un opéra.*

d. *Quel vin va __________ le mieux avec ce plat ?*

e. *Je vais vous _________ le vin.*

Solutions on page 96.

QUIZ SOLUTIONS

p.24: 1) a. True, b. False, c. True, d. True. **2)** a. *vanille*, b. *rouget*, c. *quiche*, d. *haricot*. **3)** a3, b4, c1, d2.

p.42: 1) a4, b1, c2, d3. **2)** a. *passer*, b. *casser*, c. *éviter*, d. *renverser*, e. *inviter*. **3)** a. *ore*, b. *tru*, c. *fus*, d. *gal*.

p.60: 1) a3, b4, c1, d2. **2)** d, c, e, f, b, a. **3)** a3, b4, c1, d5, e2.

p.78: 1) a3, b4, c5, d2, e1. **2)** a. *une langue-de-chat* is a biscuit not a cake, b. *les asperges* don't have shells, c. *le pain perdu* is not a dish named after a famous person. d. *un café crème* is a drink, not a dessert. **3)** a. *spécialité*, b. *typique*, c. *comment*, d. *dedans*, e. *ingrédients*.

p.95: 1) a. False, b. True, c. True, d. False. **2)** a. *ola*, b. *lère*, c. *vie*, d. *ib*. **3)** a. *débarrasser*, b. *expliquer*, c. *manger*, d. *aller*, e. *servir*.

SERIES EDITOR: **PAM BOURGEOIS**
MANAGING EDITOR: **KARI MASSON**
ARTISTIC DIRECTOR: **STEPHANIE HINDERER**
ASSISTANT EDITORS: **ERIN TREMOUILHAC, JEAN-MARIE BEL**

PHOTO CREDITS
front cover © Sarsmis / Fotolia.com
back cover © Jacques Palut / Fotolia.com

p7 top left © FOOD-micro / Fotolia.com
p18 © Gaetan Soupa / Fotolia.com
p22-23 © Brad Pict / Fotolia.com
p32 top © FOOD-pictures / Fotolia.com
p33 © Richard Villalon / Fotolia.com
p36 top © L. Santilli / Fotolia.com
p42 © Jennifer Jane / Fotolia.com
p48 © Pictures news / Fotolia.com
p52 bottom © FVLK / sxc.hu
p55 top © FOOD-micro / Fotolia.com
p61 bottom © Michael Nivelet / Fotolia.com
p66 bottom © Brad Pict / Fotolia.com
p73 top © Pictures news / Fotolia.com
p73 bottom © Chris32m / Fotolia.com
p76-77 © Jérôme Rommé / Fotolia.com
p84 top © S. Bachstroem / Fotolia.com